COAL WAS BLACK GOLD

Andrew Waters

ISBN 978-1-63961-154-6 (paperback)
ISBN 978-1-63961-155-3 (digital)

Copyright © 2023 by Andrew Waters

All rights reserved. No part of this publication may be reproduced, distributed, or transmitted in any form or by any means, including photocopying, recording, or other electronic or mechanical methods without the prior written permission of the publisher. For permission requests, solicit the publisher via the address below.

Christian Faith Publishing
832 Park Avenue
Meadville, PA 16335
www.christianfaithpublishing.com

Printed in the United States of America

1935 Jasper Alabama, a city of less than fifteen thousand in population with at least thirty-five active coal mines, and many of these mines were owned by one family, the Drummond family, with hundreds of men working day and night, extracting raw coal from the ground. Mining was hard and extremely dangerous work, but the pay for Negro men was good in 1935. Jasper is only forty miles from Birmingham, the Pittsburgh of the South, where steel mills were king of the economic success and produced excellent steel products for fifty years. Negro men were employed here in large numbers. Coal mining pay was good, and the Negro men employed in the mines of Jasper and the steel plants of Birmingham were often family men. Coal mining supported the steel plants. The coal was transported forty miles by the railroad, which also functioned with coal as the fuel for the steam engines, the iron horses that pulled the trains.

Andrew J. Waters Sr. and Mic Wright, two Negro friends, were also young elders in a Pentecostal church in Jasper, Alabama. They both lived and were employed as miners in a city with thirty-five active mines in the early 1930s. These two youthful ministers were both looking for wives: women who loved God and attended church with consistency. The Jasper church had made an announcement that there would be a holy convocation to be held in Birmingham, Alabama, at the church located in the Smithfield section of Birmingham on the last weekend of August 1941. Elder Waters had a son age five and a daughter age seven from his previous marriage. His children lived with other family members at this time.

These two young men, both divorced elders trusting God for their future, were blessed to have the last weekend in August off duty. They spent all their free time preparing to attend the holy convocation in Birmingham, Alabama, about forty miles away. The holy convocation was a conference of churches that took place early fall of each year. Church members from across the state of Alabama would gather for a seven-day-and-night series of worship services. These services consisted of community prayers, community singing, preaching, and complete fellowship with God and the people of God. The Pentecostals would celebrate God's blessing with high praise of singing and hand clapping, foot stomping, and dancing in the Holy Spirit. The fellowship spiritually and naturally was a wonderful experience for everyone.

They put their suits in the cleaners, they had their shirts laundered, and they had their Sunday shoes shined. Elder Mic Wright owned a Model T Ford automobile. He and his friend Elder Andrew J. Waters cleaned that car's inside and washed the outside and applied a little wax. That Model T looked almost new. They planned to stay the weekend, so they made an arrangement to rent rooms at a Negro rooming house in Smithfield.

At the Convocation, the two Elders did not know many of the people who were in attendance from across the state of Alabama, but they did know the supervisor of the State Women's department. Ms. Netters, she knew everyone, and she knew everyone's married or unmarried status. Ms. Netters informed the two young elders that she knew two young women who were Christians and available. She arranged for two friends, Ms. Louise Roberts and Ms. Grace Lacey, to meet these two dashing, young elders at supper.

The four met. Elder Mic Wright met Louise Roberts and fell in love on sight. Elder Andrew Waters met Grace Lacey, and they fell in love very quickly. The couples planned their marriages after their short engagements. The two ministers returned to Jasper and the mines. The two women returned to

Huntsville to their employment. Grace Lacey was employed by the retired ambassador of Dublin, Ireland. They begged Grace not to marry and leave Huntsville. Louise left her employment at the shirt laundry.

These women decided to move to Jasper with their husbands. Grace had four children from a previous marriage, ages nine, eight, five, and two. This was a difficult time for Grace, but she prayerfully prevailed, renewed her covenant with the Lord, and changed some family ties. Louise had no children, but some of her family were Muslims. Louise Wright was a tall dark brown–skinned woman, with a round pretty face. She had dimples when she smiled. Grace Waters was copper brown–skinned, small-frame woman, with long shoulder-length hair, and an inviting smile that made everyone she met feel comfortable in her presence.

On the last Sunday morning in October 1940 at 11:00 a.m., Minister Elder Mic Wright and Minister Elder Andrew Waters both showed up at one of the Sunday morning worship services at the church where Pastor Netters was pastor and his wife, Ms. Netters, were. At the end of Sunday school, Pastor Netters announced that the order of service would be changed that Sunday morning. Waiting outside were two brides-to-be and the two grooms. The musicians began to play the "Here Comes the Bride" song. The two brides began walking down the aisle. The grooms entered with the pastor and Ms. Netters from the front of the church. Everyone was fondly surprised.

After the double wedding, everyone packed to go to Jasper, Alabama, that small coal mining city about seventy-six miles east of Huntsville but close to Chattanooga, Tennessee.

Elder Andrew Waters stood about five feet, six inches in height and weighed about one hundred and fifty pounds of all muscles. Elder Waters had thick dark-brown hair; his complexion was light brown. His friend Elder Mic Wright was six feet four. Elder Wright's complexion was exceptionally light-skinned, he had straight black hair, and he weighed about two hundred and fifty pounds of muscle. These friends were coal miners, and they continued working in the Jasper coal mines for several years. Exceedingly difficult and extremely hard, working in the mines was the only choice for these churchmen and family men.

Both men continued their employment in the Jasper and Pell City mines after they were both married, but they did not know that their wives were constantly doing intercessory prayers daily for their husbands to discover employment outside of the mines. The mines were extremely dangerous. Many people were injured in the mines daily. Elder M. Wright secured employment in Pennsylvania at a steel plant near Norristown. Elder Wright and his wife left Jasper, Alabama, and the coal mines to move north.

Shortly after Elder M. Wright moved north to Pennsylvania, Elder A. Waters found employment at the Norfolk, Virginia, naval base. He, his wife, and children moved to Norfolk, Virginia. The two friends lost track of each other for ten or fifteen years. Both elders did ministry in the neighborhoods where they lived. Both wives worked by the sides of their husbands in ministry. Elder Mic Wright and Elder Andrew Waters were close friends and had experienced similar upbringings in the South, some good times and some hard times, because of racial issues. These two friends shared a mixed-race background, Negro and Caucasian, and they often experienced hostilities from both sides but more negativity from Caucasians.

Growing up and becoming men in the South helped make them determined to succeed in life. The state of Alabama where Elder Mic Wright spent his youth and became an adult was filled with problems because of his appearance. Elder Mic Wright looks like a six-foot Italian male, but he was Black. Elder Wright's appearance was his heritage that came from his parents. His father was a tall light-complected man, and his mother was a tall tan-complected woman. His origin was an extremely negative situation that had happened to the women in his family. Elder Wright's grandfather was working out of town. There were only Grandma Elizabeth Wright, Aunt Bessie, and Aunt

Gloria at the Wright home on a Saturday night, cooking, cleaning, and sewing. Sometime later, the Wright women heard a noise outside as they were preparing for Sunday and getting ready for bed. They heard many automobiles near their home. They quickly turned off all the lights. Someone forced the front door open. Men broke in and forcibly entered the house. They were called Night Riders.

The Night Riders assaulted all the Wright women brutally. Only Grandma Elizabeth Wright became pregnant. When Grandpa James Wright returned home, the Wright women told him all that had transpired. All the Wright women had to receive medical treatment from hospital staff. The country doctor was called, but he could not file a medical report at the hospital, so the police were not called.

A report would endanger the lives of the entire family. The assaults were brutal because they knew their assailants and how the legal system treated the colored people: they did not report the savage assaults. This was December 1900 in South Alabama near Mobile. The Night Riders were reported; no names were mentioned, no investigation, so nothing was done to the men who did the assaults. Grandpa Wright and Grandma Wright raised Mic with all the Wright children. Mic Wright was the product of this situation. The Wright family were light-skinned, but only Elder Mic Wright had the straight hair. Much of his life he spent trying to explain that he was Black despite his hair texture and his exceptionally light skin.

Elder Andrew Waters had almost the same youthful problem growing up in Louisiana and Mississippi. Elder Waters's father and mother were both of light complexion. Elder Waters's father was drowned six months before his birth. His mother married again to a dark-complected man, Mr. Woods. This husband and stepfather loved his two daughters but did not like Elder Waters, his stepson, who ran away before he was a teenager. He lived with cousins and friends and became independent and on his own most of his grown-up life. He has always been a hard worker, independent and fully able to take care of himself at an early age. He could pick a hundred pounds of cotton in four or five hours. He had a cousin named Paul whom he would compete with, working, dating the girls, and going to church. These two young men would always excel in all that they did, and they were excellent at picking cotton and all types of farming. These two cousins were youthful in age but mature and zealous workers. They would challenge themselves to succeed.

Elder Mic Wright and Mrs. Louise Wright had one son who died shortly after birth. After the death of their son, Elder Wright received a promotion from the corporation who owned the steel mill where he was employed near Norristown, Pennsylvania. He accepted this new employment promotion. Elder Wright and Mrs. Wright moved to Baltimore, Maryland. Shortly after moving to Baltimore, one of the leading bishops of the COGIC Pentecostal Church in Baltimore, Maryland, where Elder Wright was affiliated, appointed Elder Wright as pastor to a small church in a rural community neighborhood called Solomon's Island, about sixty miles outside of Baltimore, Maryland. Elder Wright pastored that church more than forty years. Elder and Mrs. Wright bought a beautiful home in Baltimore, Maryland.

The Wrights became very committed and active with the greater Maryland Pentecostal Churches. It was at one of these meetings in the early 1950s, at a large conference during the offering time, Elder Mic Wright and Sister Louise Wright were walking to the offering table. They were recognized by their friends Elder and Mrs. Waters, and as soon as Elder and Mrs. Waters were able to get through the crowd, they contacted the Wrights, exchanged addresseses and phone numbers, and made plans to meet each other again.

Elder Mic and Mrs. Louise Wright did not know that the Waters family had increased by two since they were last in fellowship. Elder and Mrs. Waters had two children since they were last together: a daughter and son under the age of five. The Wrights wanted to visit the Waters family in Pennsylvania.

Elder and Mrs. Waters began to prepare their recently rented small three-bedroom house.

The Waters family received a phone call from their eldest daughter saying she was on her way to Pennsylvania from Alabama and traveling with her infant son. She would need a place to stay until she was able to secure lodging. During this time, Mrs. Waters was at the Rent Control Board paying the rent. She was informed that her family was paying too much rent. The rent control immediately contacted the owner to inform them of the mistake. The owners were offended and immediately had the Waters family evicted.

The owners insisted that the Waters family vacate their property that day. The Jones/Pressley family, who owned properties in the neighborhood, heard of the eviction, and they offered to rent a small three-room house that had been used to store tools. Mr. Jones/Pressley told his nephew to remove the tools. The Waters family went to the house to clean and prepare for moving that evening. A husband, a wife, two teenage boys, an adult daughter and her child, and two children under five were busy packing and preparing to move across the street from a six-room house to a three-room house. Half of the furniture had to be placed outside under some type of protective covering.

The very same weekend, the Wright family came to visit the Waters family. Elder and Mrs. Waters secured overnight lodging for their guests in the beautiful homes of their affluent friends. They had a wonderful fellowship. The Wrights met all of the children as they had only seen the two teenage male children. The Wrights and the Waters families talked and laughed until late at night. Mrs. Waters and Elder Waters explained what had happened on such short notice. They explained what preparations they had secured. Elder Wright and his wife would not go; they wanted to stay with their friends. Mrs. Louise Wright stated that they didn't come to visit the affluent friends of the Waters family. She said to Mrs. Waters, if she sleeps on the table that she would get on the table with her friend and sleep. That was a great weekend for the Wrights and the Waters families, eating, sleeping, and going to church. Ten people in a three-room house for three days and nights in harmony.

Only Elder Mic Wright, Sister Louise Wright, Elder A. J. Waters, and Mrs. Grace Waters understood the close ties of these two families. These two men were just like blood brothers. They had shared many experiences working for the Drummond Family Corporation coal mines in both Jasper, Alabama, and Pell City coal mining operations. The Drummond Family Corporation owned many of the mining operations in the two Alabama towns. The mining operations was one of only a few places Black men in the 1930s and 1940s could make a good living, but they were not paid the same as the White men they worked with, and they were always given the most difficult tasks and the most dangerous assignments. These two brotherlike men were successful miners.

Their wives were constantly trying to get them to find other employment. In the mines, there were almost daily cave-ins and underground explosions. Men were injured daily, and many were killed, doing their jobs according to regulations. This danger, and sometimes mistreatment, did not weaken these friendships. The steel mill operations in Birmingham, Alabama in the 1940' revival only Pittsburgh. Pennsylvania, a steel producing City. These two brothers like friends continued working in those mines, to support their wives and families that depended on them.

The mining employment would continue for several years. The wives continued to pray and make comfortable homes for these two hardworking, brotherlike friends. One day, there was a cave-in in one of the mines where Elder Waters and Elder Wright were working. There were many cave-ins, but this one was greater than all the others before. All the miners were told to evacuate the mines immediately, and as the last miner ran out of the last deep tunnel, it seemed as if there was a landslide. It appeared that part of a nearby mountain's mining shaft had caved in. No lives were lost, but there were many injuries.

The fire department arrived, and many ambulances to carry the injured to the local hospitals. The news of the cave-in traveled fast, and both wives made there their way to the mines. The wives insisted that their husbands quit that day. They told their husbands that the Lord would make a way, and they were very thankful the lives of both husbands were saved.

The next twenty or thirty years, these two families sealed their relationships with visits. The Wrights would come to Harrisburg, Pennsylvania, and the Waters would visit the Wrights in Baltimore, Maryland.

Elder Mic Wright and Elder Andrew Waters fished together, hunted together, and involved themselves in many activities together, but they did not pursue coal mining again. The wives sewed together, cooked together, shopped together, washed clothes and ironed together, and solved family and church-related problems together. For almost fifty years, these two godly families stood together through all types of situations, and they managed to overcome successfully with harmony. The Wrights and the Waters lived seventy-five miles apart for almost fifty years, but they functioned as if they lived next door to each other. At any time on noticeably short notice, they were at the other friend's home middle of the week or weekend. They spiritually and socially connected.

One might think two ex-coal miners who moved into two great states like Pennsylvania and West Virginia, where coal mining was very big in the 1760 and up until the early 1970's. The coal mining was fueled by the iron industry since the early 1700s. Western Maryland also had coal mines since the 1830s that was in the George Creek Field area. The two friends had a full knowledge of the location of their surroundings, but they never returned to the mines.

Elder Waters found employment at the Olmstead Air Force Base, in Middletown, Pennsylvania. From 1951 until 1961, he was employed as a furnace stoker and fireman maintaining exceptionally large furnaces in many of the base buildings. He kept the airmen warm in the wintertime.

The four friends never forgot their origins in the coal mines of Pell City, Alabama, and Jasper, Alabama, where coal was their gold.

Elder Mic Wright became a pastor. He would invite Elder Waters to preach at the church that he pastored yearly during the pastor's anniversary service. This would be a long weekend: packing up for the weekend, preparing to leave Harrisburg early Sunday morning, driving to Baltimore, Maryland, eat breakfast with the Wrights, prepare to get on the road, and travel seventy miles south of Baltimore to Solomon's Island to worship at a small country church.

The church Elder Mic Wright pastored had some remarkably interesting people who belong to that congregation. The rural location gave the congregation a special flavor culturally, although it was near Baltimore city. One of the members was an undertaker. With some influence in the congregation, he seemed to desire more power. This situation caused friction with some of the other professional people in the congregation and some of the those who were farmers, construction workers, cooks, and many of labor employees. This friction was always apparent during the pastor's anniversary, during which time it appeared that some members jockeyed for visibility and power. When presentations and other honors were being displayed for the pastor and his wife, Elder Andrew Waters Sr. and Mrs. Grace Waters would often find themselves in the middle of situations where it would be necessary to negotiate harmony and peace while proceeding with the ministry of praise and worship, and honor for the honorees. Elder Andrew Waters Sr. and Elder Mic Wright had similar preaching styles. They were both fundamental, fire and brimstone, and they both had a strong delivery that was highly informative and challenging while they preach. Then they would sing in the middle of their sermon and then return to preaching their sermon.

It is hard to believe, but the Waters and the Wrights experienced a long and fruitful association and true friendship for fifty years. How do four people, so much alike and yet so different, remain so close and in an active relationship? Elder Mic Wright and Mrs. Louise became affluent, but Elder Andrew and Mrs. Grace Waters did not become as affluent.

Mrs. Louise Wright was about eighteen years younger than Mrs. Grace Waters, but they were always equal in their relationship. They cooked together, baked, fried, prepared fruits and vegetables and many types of meat. Both women were great cooks, and they enjoyed preparing large fancy meals for their families and guests, as they often have guests in their homes. Mrs. Waters had an edge on Mrs. Wright in the field of hospitality. Mrs. Waters had worked as a professional cook for several millionaire families before marrying Elder Waters.

Mrs. Waters knew everything about etiquette, service, table settings, and she was able to prepare and serve all types of food in all types of settings. Mrs. Waters could cook the best scratch biscuits you ever ate. She perfected her baking from her grandmother Carolina White Chunn, who won seven or eight blue ribbons at the world's fair. In fact, the family that her grandmother worked for allowed her to test new brands of baking powder that was sent to their homes for her approval. Two of her favorites were Clabber Girl and Calumet baking powder.

Mrs. Waters made the best desserts; she was an expert when preparing any types of hot or cold desserts. At her home, she always set the table for supper to serve her family. Mrs. Waters taught all her children how to cook and how to manage their own homes. She attempted to keep her home spotless; you could almost eat off the floors of Mrs. Waters's home. Although she often lived in homes that were a little run-down, she knew how to make them beautiful and comfortable. She loved her family and the work of the Lord and the church. She inspired the ladies in her community. Mrs. Waters had a vegetable garden yearly and planted flowers in her front yard, especially morning glory flowers. Mrs. Waters was a slim dark-brown woman, with long thin dark-brown shoulder-length hair. Mrs. Grace Waters would spend hours and hours preparing food for her guests. She often had guests at her home for supper, especially when her friends Elder and Sister Wright were coming to spend the weekend or when the Wrights would make one of their often one-day trips from Baltimore, Maryland, to Harrisburg, Pennsylvania, to visit the Waters family.

One Friday evening, the Waters family was visiting the Wright family, and they unimanually decided to have their evening meal at a family restaurant. The Wrights drove the lead car, and the Waters family followed. They parked their cars in the parking lot, went in the restaurant, and were seated. Some came running into the restaurant, ran into the kitchen, injured one of the cooks, and ran back out, in a matter of seconds. The Wrights and the Waters families wondered what had just happened. In a few minutes, the police arrived. No one moved out of their seats. The police officers did some interviews and left us. The Waters and the Wright families ordered their food, they ate, enjoyed their evening out, had enough to have laughter, discussed the evening actions, and how God delivered them in health. They prayed and had one of the best times of their lives. In the Bible days, Paul and Salus were locked in jail, and at midnight, they sang and prayed. God sent an earthquake of deliverance, and the jailer and all his household were saved.

Mrs. Wright had a lot in common with Mrs. Waters; how they achieved their dreams was different, but they both loved beautiful things. Mrs. Wright had an incredibly beautiful home; she was able to afford a maid. Mrs. Louise Wright was spoiled by her husband. Elder Wright was twenty-five years older than her, but they were truly in love with each other. Mrs. Wright spent many years as a shirt finisher in several laundries, but when she married Elder Wright, he did not want her to work, and she became a homemaker. She was very involved in the work of the local church, district church, and the jurisdiction church of Maryland.

Mrs. Louise Wright was a good cook, but she did not like cooking and servings as much as her friend, Mrs. Waters. These two close friends were so much alike when together, but quite different apart. Grace and Louise both had a common background working in laundries as shirt finishers (pressing them perfectly). In the laundry business, anyone who developed that skill became a valuable employee in the dry cleaning business. Louise's working career included clerical work, but most of her employment career was spent in service of private homes: cooking, cleaning, also acting as a nanny. When Grace left the laundry business, she became a private home technician. Grace said she desired receiving her wages daily. Grace had four children at home that she was concerned about.

Often Grace would take in other relatives. For a short time, her brother came to live in their small home, then later her mother came to live with her a short while. Grace and Louise were both great homemakers, great church workers and married to ministers whom they supported at home and at church. Grace and Louise served their churches and communities in many capacities. They were completely involved in their homes and the work of the Lord, women with full commitments to their purpose. These two remarkably close friends went through many situations with locked arms and determination, faced any economic difficulty, family problems, and world-changing situations. Grace and Louise remained constant. Grace Waters and Louise Wright assisted many young women; they taught them how to care for themselves, their husbands, their children, their homes, and the importance of loving God and being a good homemaker.

The appearance of the two coal miner ministers could be compared to the old comic strip Mutt and Jeff. Mic Wright was over six feet tall, and Andrew Waters was five feet six. Yet one could not separate these two friends. They loved to talk about those difficult times and how they were able to overcome great difficulties and succeed. Mic would talk about the time he tried to make some biscuits for their breakfast; the biscuits were extremely hard and uneatable. Mic and Andrew decided to throw the hard biscuit into a pig pen that was not far from their dwelling. Both men began to laugh and laugh. They said the pigs would not eat the biscuits. Andrew could cook and had held several jobs as a short order and a heavy-duty cook before the friends met. Mic never learned to cook a lick.

Who would have thought that two Alabama coal mine ministers would form such a close brotherhood bond that would last and last? Elder Wright and Elder Waters had many discussions concerning race relations from the 1930s, '40s, '50s, '60s, and '70s. These two friends seem to have a deep understanding of human behavior. Neither had an academic education in human behaviors, psychology or sociology, but they knew human behaviors very well. They always had a reasonable solution for many situations and offered their assistance to many of their fellow neighbors and in the churches where they both were excellent pastors, where mother wit and good common senses were valued and obeyed.

They had wholesome strategies that were helpful in work situations and home and family situations. As ministers, they held some astounding Bible discussions. Together they prayed often for the world, their families, their communities, and for the people they pastored. They filled both homes with constant prayer, praise, and true worship. Their behavior together was always reverent and kind. Never did two men of limited academic background display a love for God and family, whenever they met. I believe that both had attended the tenth grade in high school and studied in some of the federal programs that were provided by President Franklin Delano Roosevelt's administration.

For fifty years, four saintly people—Elder Mic, Sister Louise Wright, Elder Andrew, and Sister Grace Waters—enjoyed a close, spiritual, and natural relationship. This relationship continued throughout hospitalizations, pain, sickness, and death; nothing brought about a change to these loving friends. Elder Mic Wright, the oldest member of this group, became ill and was put into the John Hopkins Hospital, where he was diagnosed to have terminal cancer. After a long hospital stay, Elder Wright fell asleep in the arms of Jesus Christ, leaving a greatly saddened threesome. Now aging Louise Wright, without the love of her life, continued with her two lifetime friends.

One of the sons of Elder and Sister Waters stated that he had never personally witnessed a relationship shared by the Wrights and the Waters families. It's almost unbelievable how well they got along and interacted regularly. Going to the Wrights' home on Bent Lou Street, just off North Avenue in Baltimore, Maryland, the Waters would share old and new information for hours and hours. Their information was never about others; it was their own experiences, the Lord's deliverance, and the laughable things that happened to them when apart and those things that happened when they were together.

Can you believe this? Elder and Mrs. Waters had four sons that Elder and Mrs. Wright were involved with, from their youth until they were grown men, and they continued with an active and close relationship throughout the lives of these sons, their wives, and children. They were like an uncle and aunt to all the Waters children. When one of the Waters sons endured a divorce, Elder and Mrs. Wright became so concerned that they arranged for that son to meet one of Baltimore's leading pastor's daughters, Deborah Tally, who was the daughter of Pastor James Tally Sr. Deborah was a very good musician, and she played the Hammond organ. Deborah was a beautiful young lady with thick long hair, and she also had experienced an unhappy divorce. Deborah Tally was the oldest daughter in the Tally family.

Pastor Elder James Tally was the pastor of a small church in Baltimore. Elder Tally, although small in stature, was a giant in kindness who was married to Mrs. Tally: a saintly woman, and an exceptionally good pianist who played during worship service in the church. The Tally family consisted of Pastor James Tally Sr., Mrs. Tally, James Tally Jr. who was also a musician, and Lydia, the youngest daughter who could sing. The Tally family loved the Lord and were close friends of Elder and Mrs. Wright. The Wright family was blessed with some wealth and were generous to their church and their friends. The Wrights had several cars: a new Lincoln and a Ford Fairlane.

They would not get rid of that old Ford. Although it was a 1955, it functioned like that new 1972 Lincoln. Mrs. Wright kept that old Ford long after the death of her husband and would often drive it more than the new Lincoln.

The harmonious friendship of the Waters and the Wrights extended far beyond what is commonly called friendship. These four people supported each other in everything: sickness of family members, divorce of family members, and many tragedies, but the awesome four always came out on the top of every situation. The Wrights and the Waters defined the Christian family by many examples of godly living, embracing truth, love, and respect for everyone.

Sometime after Mrs. Wright's death, Elder Waters and Mrs. Waters's health also deteriorated. Mrs. Waters fell ill and was the next of the four friends to die. Mrs. Grace Waters had been a great woman of prayer, faith, and work. She almost never raised her voice. She believed and trusted God in all things. The fact of the matter is Elder and Mrs. Waters had held street meetings all over South Central Pennsylvania for about ten years in the early 1950s and '60s, in addition to assisting her husband when he was called to pastor in Both Williamsport, Pennsylvania, and Mount Union, Pennsylvania.

Elder Waters was sent to Williamsport, Pennsylvania, by Senior Bishop Oroz T. Jones. Elder Waters and his wife and family were sent there to help a small mission with a Mother Brown and her daughter, Ella Mae. Elder Waters, Mrs. Waters, and the children made great sacrifices. For three years, they traveled eighty-four miles one way to minister in this old railroad city. After three years, Bishop O. T. Jones senior called Pastor Andrew Waters to reassign him to Mount Union, Pennsylvania. Bishop Jones sent Elder Waters to pastor the Tabernacle COGIC in the town of Mount Union, Pennsylvania. Mount Union had a large active brick yard that employed many hardworking Negro men, and the Negro women were employed at a women's dressmaking factory where many belonged to Tabernacle church.

Tabernacle COGIC had a long history of difficulty being pastored by anyone. Some of the great pastors who had pastored through the years before Elder Andrew Waters arrived were Elder Wyoming Wells, Elder Moses Griffin, and others. The membership was good and growing but always with contention. There were many large families attending Tabernacle church, but after graduation, most of the graduates would leave town and never return to live in Mount Union.

This situation was not too disturbing to Elder Waters; he could rely on his friend Elder Wright coming to visit him with Mrs. Wright on his arm. These preachers supported each other in almost everything in ministry. In the mid-1960s, a call from Bishop O.T. Jones Jr to Elder Waters appointed him as pastor of Ashley Tabernacle COGIC, in Columbia, Pennsylvania: a Lancaster County where he pastored until retiring in the early 1990s after a number of years before his family were able to convince him to consider retirement. Elder Andrew J. Waters Sr. was given the opportunity to organize the Susquehanna Valley District of the COGIC, Commonwealth jurisdiction. Elder Andrew J. Waters Sr. served as the Susquehanna Valley District superintendent for eighteen years; Elder Waters selected Mother Catherine Walker as his district missionary. Mother C. Walker, the wife of Deacon Ralph Walker, were members of the Emanuel COGIC in York, Pennsylvania, and Elder Walter Wise was their pastor.

Elder Mic Wright preached at many of Elder Waters's pastoral anniversary services, and Elder Andrew J. Waters preached the closing sermon at Elder Mic Wright's pastoral anniversary services on Solomon's Island some sixty miles outside of Baltimore, Maryland. Elder Wright was overjoyed when he discovered his friend had become one of the organizers of the Commonwealth of Pennsylvania Jurisdiction COGIC State, baptizing in the Susquehanna River at the Columbia, Pennsylvania, boat dock. Both men and their wives nearing retiring time, they had become worn out in the service of the Lord; they did not want to rust out.

When Mrs. Waters's children became sick, prayer was administered first, then she used her medical books and took them to the hospital. She was a woman of determination. Sister Grace Waters's greatest achievements were the revivals that she ran. The revival at Lumpkin temple yielded ten souls that were baptized by Elder Julius Lumpkin and Elder Belgium Baxter. A youth revival produced twelve born-again souls at the Faith Chapel COGIC that Mrs. Waters led.

The Wrights would come to Harrisburg to visit Elder and Mrs. Waters and accompany them on hospital visits and home visits to the sick and shut-in. This behavior was repeated when the Waters went to Baltimore; the ministry for and to the people never stop.

Sister Grace homemaking skills were transposing the back to the front. She would redo a falling down shack and create it into a palace of beauty. Mrs. Grace was quite the decorator; with few resources, she would make the back into a front, with style and beauty for everyone to enjoy. She had a desire to live in a new home. She worked and inspired her husband to purchase a new home for her family.

She would inspire her husband to visit his family, which he had not seen for thirty-five years nor been in contact with. She would write letters to his family who appreciated her letters, but they desired to hear from him. She saved her money and planned a visit to his family after a thirty-five year or more absence. What a family healing. Many family members had died, and many new births had occurred.

The love that was experienced from the friendship of the Wright family healed, secured, and renewed the Waters family. Mrs. Waters spent her entire lifetime healing naturally and spiritually wherever and whenever possible. Mrs. Waters was an expert peacemaker, and her friend Mrs. Louise Wright also practiced the art of peacemaking at home and at church. Once in a while, Ms. Louise Wright did not feel like being a host after inviting the Waters family to her home. No matter what the situation, they worked it out in a loving, friendly, and respectable way. The relationship that these four believing friends had seemed almost fictional. But it was real and true. Sometimes the things God does in our lives and in the lives of believers seem small, but the impact on the lives of those people watching and hoping and seeking to have the favor of God can be found in our everyday lives: the way we treat each other, especially when we demonstrate true mercy to those who have made bad life decisions. Every time there was a crisis in the Wright home, somehow the Waters family knew it, and they would make an unannounced, unplanned visit seventy-five miles to Baltimore, Maryland, with prayerful words and comfort.

Whenever a phone call of any trouble in the Waters family home, very shortly the response would be answered with a knock at the door (day or night), the Wrights had traveled to Harrisburg, Pennsylvania, and always had a prayerful thought and often a solution to the problem. The entire world didn't have to know the family's personal business. In those early days, there were many problems. The Waters had a blended family of various age groups, and they often tested their parents, but always becoming subject to family decisions and what the Bible said the outcome should be. "Ye shall know the truth and the truth shall make you free," a Bible verse both families lived by.

Elder Mic Wright would always tell on her, he would give away her secret laziness tendencies, but the four of them would have a big laugh. Mrs. Waters would go into the kitchen and assist her friend although she was her invited guest. The four of them always discovered a method or way to resolve their differences. Every time the Wrights and the Waters got together, they would part with a long prayer, in a circle, with everyone holding hands, often the two women's eyes would fill with tears of joy, hugs, and kisses.

Two successful Negro coal miner ministers were able to progress in an environment and an unfriendly society in the south and in the north. These two men and their supporting wives achieved success in spite of all the pain in a society that did not embrace them. They found faith and truth in humanity;

they also found hope, and their love for God was their reward. Those experiences, some dangerous and death threatening, drew these coal miners to their goal of life, which can be defined *black gold*.

Elder Andrew Waters and some of his friends in the Harrisburg, Pennsylvania, area founded a tradesman guild consisting of Negro plumbers, electricians, carpenters, concrete finishers, and brick/stone masons in the late 1950s. This was almost unheard of for Negro men to achieve as organized professionals being led off themselves. This inspiration came from Mrs. Waters, Mr. and Mrs. Wright, and other friends and encouraged Elder Waters to pursue his dreams. Elder Waters, Mrs. Waters, Elder Wright, and Mrs. Wright gave God the glory and honor for all their successes. Elder Andrew Waters did not inform many people that he had been blessed to attend a night school, a federal government school, the WPA school that President Roosevelt and his cabinet started, where he learned to do carpentry, cement finishing, brick laying, and without attending other classes, he would watch on his lunch time, and he taught himself how to repair automobiles, fix electric sockets, and plumbing.

Elder Waters discovered that some of the people from the North did not believe in the knowledge and training that Southern Negro men had received, especially when they came to the northern states. This educational information he would only share with his financial sponsors. Those experiences and lessons learned by Elder Waters and Elder Wright in those damp, dark, dangerous mines of Alabama were positive experiences to draw from.

Elder Waters introduced his longtime friend Elder Wright to his Harrisburg preacher friends and work friends, and they shared and enjoyed old family stories. They also had a friend who was close to both. He was a little slow of understanding, but everyone who knew Brother Jack protected him from outsiders making fun of him. They loved to tell one story about Brother Jack becoming a believer. Brother Jack wanted to attend a revival that was going on in Chattanooga, Tennessee. Another friend who was about the same size as Brother Jack offered to loan the brother a new serge suit that he had recently purchased.

All these friends got ready for church. They arrived at the beginning prayer time, so they all kneeled to pray. The brother who loaned the suit to Brother Jack asked him to get up and not to kneel in his new suit, he said this loudly. Brother Jack got up very embarrassed and feeling bad. Later the same week, Brother Jack wanted to attend the revival very badly because he had just become a new believer. A second friend heard about the situation, and he offered to help by lending Brother Jack a suit. Brother was so nervous when it was prayer time; everyone knelt to pray. Brother Jack stood as everyone knelt to pray.

This second friend looked at Brother Jack and said, "Get down on it. That suit is bought and paid for." Everyone had a big laugh and welcomed Elder Mic Wright and Elder Waters into Harrisburg Preacher Friend group. The group told many funny stories, and all had clean fun, laughing.

The first real sadness for this foursome began with the illness of Elder Mic Wright. Elder Wright's sickness seemed to come upon him suddenly. Elder Wright never complained. Sometimes you could see the terrible pain in his body, and he never would say a word, but when you looked into his face, especially his eyes, you could see the pain and suffering this old preacher pastor was going through. On many occasions, the Waters family would visit Elder Mic Wright in the John Hopkins Hospital in Baltimore. Elder Mic Wright was extremely sick. His sickness was very devastating for his wife and his church congregation. They lived a long distance outside of Baltimore, but they were there often lending their support to Elder Wright's wife, Mrs. Louise Wright. Truth is everyone became closer together, assisting and doing ministry. Mrs. Wright held the church together, although she never called herself a preacher.

The Waters family would drive to Baltimore to pick up Mrs. Louise Wright, and then all would go and visit Elder Mic Wright. These visits were incredibly sad; you could see Elder

Wright's life slowly leaving his body. Mrs. Wright and other visitors would stay in the room, praying and visiting. One day, the Waters family received the call from Mrs. Wright that Elder Mic Wright had expired. The families prepared for a great homegoing service. Some felt joy but some deep sadness; the four was now three. In later years, one by one, a different member of the four would leave the others behind. The last to leave was Elder Andrew J. Waters Sr. He fought a good fight, and he kept the faith until the end. He left peacefully in his sleep.

There was a special event the Waters family was involved in shortly after the death of Elder Mic Wright. Mrs. Louise Wright was yet grieving the loss of her beloved husband. No one wanted Mrs. Louise Wright to drive alone from Baltimore, Maryland, to Harrisburg, Pennsylvania. How she found out about the event, no one knows, but she drove by herself and was a part of the event, and everyone was blessed with her appearance.

There has never been a family so godly and with strong family ties that lasted almost sixty years, with consistency in Bible-believing, trust, concern, and support on all levels. How could four nonprofessional men and women be propelled to such glorious heights in society and wonderful spiritual heights in the church? Elder Waters, as a young minister once, was the person who carried the briefcase of our founding father of the COGIC, Bishop Charles Harrison Mason.

The method of ordination that Bishop C.H. Mason used was often questioned. Many of the older and younger ministers would seek to assist Bishop Mason, some of the younger ones were attending Saints Junior College, and others had a desire to learn ministry from the founding father of the COGIC. A group of young men and older men were walking through Mason Temple. Bishop Mason stopped and turned to Andrew Waters Sr., who was carrying his briefcase. He said, "Son, have you been ordained yet?"

Andrew Waters said, "No, sir."

Bishop Mason laid his hands on Andrew Waters's head and said, "You are ordained an elder in the COGIC," then he continued to proceed walking through Mason Temple. The Wrights and the Waters never would seek church, office, praise, or promotion. Everything that happened to them was thrust upon them through leadership. Like Joseph, you can go from the dungeon pit, to the palace, without seeking to be promoted. The Waters and the Wrights were the coal miners full of praise and worship who found gold in true relationships with their God and their fellow men. They served their God, their church, and their community until their death.

"And Pharaoh said unto Joseph, Forasmuch as God hath Shewed thee all this, there is none so discreet and wise as thou art: Thou shalt be over my house, and according unto thy word shall all my people be ruled: only in the throne will I be greater than thou" (Genesis 41:39–40 KJV).

ABOUT THE AUTHOR

The son of Pastor Andrew J. Waters Sr. and Evangelist Grace L. Waters

A family man and father of two children

Entrepreneur, educator, writer, Bible student, composer, and curriculum designer

Attended Roger Williams University, Bristol, Rhode Island (Criminal Justice)

Bachelors of science Edinboro University of PA (secondary education social studies)

Attended Pittsburgh Theological Seminary, PGH, Pennsylvania (Divinity)

Masters of Science Phoenix University, adult education, Phoenix, Arizona

Traveled as a foreign, missionary, and gospel singer, nationally and internationally

www.ingramcontent.com/pod-product-compliance
Lightning Source LLC
Chambersburg PA
CBHW021001180526
45163CB00006B/2449